THE TRIP

By Pat Birtwistle

Illustrations by Bradley Moore

Patnor Publishing

ACKNOWLEDGMENTS

A heartfelt thanks to Pat Nelson (my friend and research consultant) for her help and encouragement, Nick Sidoti for his enthusiasm, wealth of ideas and insights; Ann Marie Crocco for allowing the students in her school to pilot these novelettes, Angela Marcov who piloted these novelettes and showed such enthusiasm, and to Carole McGregor and Judy Metler for their editing skills. And a special thanks to Paul Dayboll, Linda Roote and Bradley Moore for their help with how to best get these books printed and for creating our website.

Above all, a very special thanks to Norm, my husband and best friend, for all his hard work in making these books become a reality.

THE TRIP

By Pat Birtwistle

Illustrations by Bradley Moore

THE TRIP

CHAPTER 1

The Trip

Kim couldn't help it. She had made a pact with the kids. She felt badly that she had let them down. They had not asked her why she went to the junk yard that day. They did not tell on her when she got into trouble. The rest of the kids had just helped her. She wanted to make it up to them, but she could not think of a way to do that. "Maybe one day I can help them. Why do I want so badly to get rich?" she asked herself.

"I have hurt the kids and would have hurt my folks too, if the kids had told them. I will just have to cool it from now on and stay out of trouble. That's it! No more wanting to be rich!"

The rest of the kids did not tell Kim's folks because they had big plans for the days to come. There was a bus trip. They had told their folks, and they wanted to go. But they had been in so much trouble that they did not think that their folks would let them go.

"Can I help you with that, Mom?" Nick was asking. "You could have a rest and I'll do that for you."

Bob was helping out too, as were the rest of the kids. They wanted so badly to go on that trip to the farm. They wanted to go horseback riding.

Soon, the day came when they had to pay for the trip. Would their folks let them go?

"No!" said Beth's mom.

"No!" all the moms said.

"But it is just a day trip. We could not get into trouble on a farm. We will just go riding. How can we get into trouble? We have kept out of trouble for some time now." The folks did not find out that Kim had been in big trouble at the junk yard. "Can we go? Can we? All the kids are going," the kids begged.

The kids kept asking. They kept pushing their folks. At last they won. The kids had made a pact. If their folks let them go, they would stay out of trouble. But that was not to be. Again, trouble would find them.

They took their food for the day and as the bus left the block, Bob's mom asked, "Do you think that they will be OK? Those kids do seem to find trouble. These days I get upset when they go out."

As they were waving goodbye to the kids, Nick's mom said, "They are good kids. They just seem to get into things by not thinking. But, I think they should be OK this time."

*　　*　　*　　*　　*

The folks were a little upset by all the things that went on with their kids that summer. Summer was coming to an end, and they wanted the kids to have some fun.

When they got to the farm, the kids said that they would have a good day with no trouble. They wanted to ride all day, but the farmer just had a few horses, and there were a lot of kids. So some of the kids had to find something to do for some time. They went into the barn to have a look.

"Let's go up the steps to the top of the barn and see what is up there," said Dan. Some of the kids liked that.

As they were going up the steps, one kid fell. He fell with a thud. Beth and the rest of the kids ran over to see if he was hurt. The boy lay still. At last, he sat up with some help. He was badly winded but not hurt.

Beth went over to Dan and asked, "What were you thinking? You led the kids up there. What are you going to do, get us into more trouble? Dan, I'm so mad at you!" she said as she left the barn to tell the rest of the kids.

Now Dan was mad. He was just trying to have some fun. Dan was thinking, "Why did Beth have to get so upset? It was not as if we are little kids or something. Beth just wants things her way all the time. She did not have to tell the rest of the kids. She put me down. I'll get back at her for that!"

CHAPTER 2

At The Pool

The kids were all mad at Dan. They wanted to have fun, but not his way. They left the barn and went out back. There was a pool there. This pool was not for swimming. It was where the horses came for water. They went down the path to the pool and began pitching things into the water. There was lots of stuff to pitch. The kids would not look at Dan because they were so mad at him.

They had to cool it, or one of them would say something to him.

After a time, Nick said, "You have to see this." He was by the water and looking down into it. When the kids came to have a look, Bob stepped into the water. He got stuck in the mud. Then Nick got stuck. As they came over to help, the rest of the kids kept getting stuck. Beth grabbed Nick's hand, but she could not get him out. Down they went into the water. They looked so funny. Then Kim gave Bob a push. He grabbed her and down they went.

They were having a good time in the mud. At last, they got out, but they were wet and muddy. Dan was standing way off by the barn and was thinking, "I'll get back at them before the day is over. They think they are so cool. I'll get them!"

The kids were not to ride before noon. They wanted to do something to fill in the time. Dan went with them but stayed way back. There was a big hill by the barn. There was a little shed at the top of the hill.

"What do you think is in that shed up there?" asked Bob.

"We could get to the top. We could rest and take a look," said Kim.

They liked that, and so Nick said, "Last one up is a rat."

As the kids were going up the hill, they pushed and tripped and, to Dan, it looked like they were having a lot of fun.

Nick led the way because he was faster. Then he stopped. He yelled, "Look out!"

The rest of the kids stopped, but they could not think of why he said that.

"What is it, Nick?" Kim asked. "Why are we stopping?"

Nick kept still and said to the rest of the kids, "There is a big snake. If it's what I think it is, it's a killer."

"Oh! No!" Beth began yelling. "I can't stand snakes! Let's get out of here!"

"Beth," Nick said softly," you are going to spook it. Be still! Stop yelling. Bob, you like snakes. Can you see the snake from where you are? Can you tell what kind it is?"

Bob said, "I can't see it from here and I do not want to spook it by coming up there. Tell me what it looks like and we will see if I can tell if it is a killer."

"It is in the pool of water, but it looks like it is all black. When the sun hits its skin, the black seems to look like all kinds of colors. I cannot tell just how big it is. It is a fat one. It looks like it is just resting in the pool of water," said Nick.

Bob said. "There is one snake that picks up colors when it is in water. Be still. From what Nick said, I think it is a killer snake and they are so fast we could all die in no time. There is no way for us to get out of this. We will have to kill it."

"But, how will we do that?" asked Kim. "We don't have anything here to kill a snake and we have to keep still or we will spook it."

"Think of something!" said Beth.

CHAPTER 3

On The Hill

Dan could see the kids stop. He could not think of why they did that. "Maybe they are up to something," he said to himself. "I'm still going to get back at them. I'll think of a way! I'll find out what they're up to." As he came up to where Bob was standing, he could see that the kids were not being funny.

Beth's skin was white, and she was looking up at the sky.

"What is it?" Dan asked Bob. Dan stayed back because by now, he could tell that there was some trouble.

Bob said, "It's a snake. It's a killer snake from what Nick told me. What do you think we should do? If we run for it, it may come after us and they are fast. It would get one of us or maybe all of us. It's big, and they are faster than we are. We were thinking we should kill it. But how? What do you think we should do? The girls do not like snakes at all. Look at them. We have to do something!"

Dan said, "All I can think of is a rock. A rock could do it. Nick is a good shot. If we could get a rock to him, I think that he could kill it. We will have to do it slowly, or we'll spook the snake. The rock will have to be a big one to do the job. But it cannot be too big or we will have trouble getting it to him."

They told Nick what they planned to do.

"No way!" Nick said. "What if I don't hit it? That will make it mad, and then it would come after me. Think of something."

The girls just kept saying, "Do something!"

Nick said, "And will you stop saying 'Do something'. That's not helping at all. Can you think of what we should do?"

"Nick, if you don't kill it, what can we do? If we go for help, we may not get back in time. You must do this!" said Bob.

Nick felt sick. He felt all the kids looking at him, but he did not want to kill it. At last, he felt that he had to try. "OK" he said.

The snake looked up at Nick. "Get a big rock up to me. I may not hit it, but I'll try."

Nick liked snakes. He did not want to kill this one, but he felt that he had to do this. Dan backed up slowly.

Little by little, he made his way down the hill. The rock he got was big, but not too big for the girls to pass it up to Nick. He picked up the rock and went back up the hill. The kids were standing still. They wanted to get this over.

"This is it," Dan said softly to Bob as he handed him the rock. Beth slowly took the rock, then passed it to Kim.

Kim could see the snake from where she was standing. She began taking the rock from Beth when she saw the snake lift its head. She stopped. "Be still!" she said softly to Beth. "The snake just looked up. It could be going in for the kill." The snake lifted its head, then lay down again. "I think it's OK now," said Nick.

They all felt sick that they had to kill it. Slowly, Kim took the rock from Beth and passed it off to Nick. She kept looking at the snake when she was doing this. She could not keep her hands still as she handed him the rock. Nick felt the way Kim did, but he did not let on.

As Dan was getting the rock and it was being passed up to him, Nick was thinking to himself, "I must do this. I must to this." He was the one who had to kill the snake before it could kill them. Thinking this, his skin felt odd but he slowly pushed the rock up over his head. He was a good shot but just how good was he? He looked down at the snake. It began to lift its head up again.

"Do it!" he said to himself.

Just then Beth let out a yell.

CHAPTER 4

The Ride

Just as Nick was going to pitch the rock at the snake and Beth let out a yell, the snake took off. The kids fell down and lay there. They did not say a thing. At last Dan asked, "Should we get back to the barn? It must be time for us to ride." He did not think of how mad he was at them before all this. They were OK and that was all he could think of now.

"Yeah," said Bob, "I think we should get back."

The kids got up and went slowly back to the barn. They were all thinking that they could have been killed. Today had begun well, but it had not stayed that way. The kids were in for just as much trouble as the day went on.

"Hey, you kids," the farmer said, "It is time for your ride. Where were you? We were looking all over for you. Come on and get a horse. That is why you came, isn't it?" He was thinking of how odd it was that the kids looked so upset, but he did not ask them why. He just helped them get up on the horses.

There was a farmhand that took the riders out. So, when the kids were on the horses, the farmer said that the kids should do what the farmhand said. Then, off they went slowly down the riding path.

It felt good to be up on horses. As they were riding, the kids felt better. The farmhand led them down the path that went into the bush. He yelled back at them, "If you stay on the path, when we are in the bush, you will be OK. Do not get off the path. The land in the bush has lots of pits and the horses trip. Just have fun and look out for snakes. Horses do not like snakes. The snakes spook the horses and they will make a run for the barn if they see a snake."

"Oh, no!" the kids were thinking. "Not snakes again!"

Beth was a good rider. She and her mom went to a farm where they had horseback riding. Kim had not been on a horse before. She felt good. The boys were thinking that they were good riders, but they, too, had not been on horses before. They wanted to go faster. They wanted to see how fast these horses could go. Dan yelled up to the farm-hand, "Can we go faster? Can we see what these horses can do?"

The farmhand looked back. He did not say a thing. He just kept going slowly down the path. Dan wanted to kick his horse in the ribs to make it run. He didn't do that because he did not want the kids to get mad at him again.

They came to the end of the path. They were making a left to go back to the barn when Bob's horse tripped. The rest of the horses jumped. The farmhand looked back just in time to see Dan land in the bushes. As he went back to help Dan, all the horses took off and were running back to the barn. Bob's horse began kicking and Bob grabbed on. He wanted to slow his horse down, but he could not think of how to do that.

Kim and the rest of the kids kept yelling at the horses to try to get them to stop. But their yelling just upset the horses more. Beth was trying to get the kids to stop yelling. The horses were running too fast for them to make out what she said.

"If I could get them to stop yelling," she was thinking, "maybe the horses would slow down. The horses are just spooked." When the farmer had seen that Beth could ride, he gave her a fast horse. "I must do something," she said to herself. "What can I do to get them to slow down? There is not much room on this path for me to pass the horses, but that is what I will have to do if I am going to help. Where is that farmhand? This is his job. Someone is going to get hurt!"

CHAPTER 5

You Can Do It!

The horses were not slowing down. The kids stayed on, but Beth could see that they would not last the rest of the way. She kicked her horse in the ribs. Her horse went off the path and ran faster when she did this. She looked back to see if the farmhand was coming to help, but he was not there. It was up to her to stop someone from getting hurt.

Beth gave her horse a good kick and said softly to it, "Come on, boy! You can do it. Get past the horses so we can slow them down."

This horse was good. It tripped now and then, but kept going. It began running like the wind. It went past one horse like a flash. It felt so good. Beth did not have to kick it again. It wanted to get back to the barn and get a rest and some water. It shot past horse after horse. At last, Beth's horse was out in the open.

She began saying softly, "Good boy! Good boy! Slow down now. Maybe the rest of the horses will slow down if you do. Whoa! That's it! Just try to stay out here in the open. Good boy!"

Beth had her horse running more slowly. The rest of the horses did not try to pass it. She had all the horses slowing down. By now, she could see the barn and the horses were still running. She had to stop them from running before they got back. If the farmer saw them running like that, the farmhand would be in trouble.

The farmhand did his job. It was just that Bob's horse had tripped and that had spooked all the horses. Beth's horse was still running, but she had it going more and more slowly.

Just before they got to the barnyard, the farmhand and his horse came running past Beth and her horse.

"Whoa," he said. When the horses saw him, they slowed down. He stopped them. "You did a good job," he said as he looked at Beth. "Dan is coming. We will stay here and when he comes, go slowly back. Then I will not get into trouble with the boss. I must keep this job. The farmer will see that the horses have been running so let's take our time getting back." By the time they came into the barn-yard, Dan was with them.

The farmer came over as they got down from the horses. "Did you kids have a good ride?" he asked. He stopped and looked at the horses. "Why are the horses all wet? They look as if they have had a good run. You kids will have to help rub them down. Let them have some water but not too much."

"You," he said to the farmhand, "come here!"

The kids did as the farmer said. They took the horses to the pool and then to the barn for a rubdown. They kept looking over to where the farmer and the farmhand were standing. They had so much trouble that summer that they did not want the farmhand to get into trouble. They could not tell if he did.

The farmer looked cross as the farmhand told him about the ride.

On the trip back home, the kids all told Beth that she was good. She was the best rider they had seen. The kids had helped her a lot, so she felt good that she could help them.

"I hurt all over," Beth said. "It hurts to help you kids!" They were thinking how funny they must have looked as they hung onto the horses running down that path!

"Now, before we get back, what are we going to tell our folks about this trip?" Nick asked.

They hurt for days but could not let on to their folks. No way.

THE TRIP

It is just a trip to a farm for horseback riding. The kids had been in so much trouble that their folks do not want them to go. At last, they let them go on the trip. The kids had made a pact that they will stay out of trouble. When they are riding, the horses get spooked. Beth had ridden a horse before, but the rest of the kids had not. The kids end up in big trouble once again.

"This is a great book. I liked it a lot."
-Thomas

"I really, really liked the part about the snake."
-Robert

ISBN 0-9733663-5-4

www.ingramcontent.com/pod-product-compliance
Lightning Source LLC
Chambersburg PA
CBHW060646030426
42337CB00018B/3475